Découpage

MILNER CRAFT SERIES

Découpage

AN ILLUSTRATED GUIDE

NERIDA SINGLETON

SALLY MILNER PUBLISHING

First published in 1991 by
Sally Milner Publishing Pty Ltd
67 Glassop Street
Birchgrove NSW 2041 Australia

Reprinted 1992

© Nerida Singleton, 1991

Production by Sylvana Scannapiego,
Island Graphics
Design by David Constable
Layout by Gatya Kelly, Doric Order
Illustrations by Alison Hill
Photography by Glenn Weiss
Typeset in Australia by Asset Typesetting Pty Ltd
Printed in Australia by Impact Printing, Melbourne

National Library of Australia
Cataloguing-in-Publication data:

Singleton, Nerida, 1948-
    Decoupage

    ISBN 1 86351 048 6.

    1. Decoupage. I. Title. (Series: Milner craft series).

745.546

Distributed in Australia by Transworld Publishers

Back cover photograph features brooches, earrings
and hair accessories by Amanda Ho.

DEDICATION

To Evan, Scott, Drew, Anna, Jaime, Julie, Belinda and Debbie.

ACKNOWLEDGEMENTS

My deepest thanks to my mother Joy Lewis, my friends Jo Harrold and Dell Ruddy, my aunt Fay MacDonald, my daughter Debbie and her husband Steven Jeppersen, and especially my husband Evan and my children, who allowed me the time to promote découpage by carrying out all my usual responsibilities for me.

My friends Joan Wotherspoon and Lorna McKay were terrific in constant crises. Myles Robins, Pamela Robins, Kevin Lewis and Irene and Don Singleton gave support and encouragement.

Special thanks to:

Mary-Ann Danaher, who caringly and professionally edited the manuscript, and supervised the colour photographs.

Glenn Weiss, whose creative photography is always wonderful, and his partner Cindy, whose dedication in the studio is immense.

Alison Hill, whose illustrations are superb.

Fae and Brian Rentoul of Noosa, who brought a new dimension to the concept of workshops in their establishment.

I'm grateful for the support and encouragement of Audrey Raymond, Lola McNickle, Diana Brandt, Glynne McGregor, Amanda Ho, Frances Robinson, and Anne Bradley and Christine Ames.

Special thanks also to Dell Ruddy, Fay Seeney, Amanda Ho and Margo Cavill for generously allowing their découpage to be included in this book.

Props for the photography were kindly loaned by Paul McDowell, Linda Carroll, Dell Ruddy and Mary-Ann Danaher.

Interviews and articles by:

Stephanie Wood of The *Courier Mail*, Brisbane;

Grace Garlick of The *Sunday Mail*, Brisbane;

Sheila Venn-Brown of *Craft and Home* magazine;

Christine Whiston of *Australian Country Craft and Decorating*; and

Pepita Dunlop of *Vogue* magazine

have created an enormous interest in découpage, and provide much inspiration.

And to Sally Milner and her Staff, thank you for allowing this work to be published.

CONTENTS

Acknowledgements   vi
Introduction   1
 1 Objects and Images   4
 2 Requirements   12
 3 Techniques
     — Preparation   16
     — Sealing   17
     — Cutting   19
     — Gluing   21
     — Varnishing   22
     — Sanding   25
 4 Finishes
     — Gloss   28
     — Wax   28
 5 Project 1 — Tablemat   30
 6 Project 2 — Box   34
 7 Project 3 — Hat Box   44
 8 Screens   49
 9 Rounded Surfaces   54
10 Antiquing   55
11 Problems and Solutions   58
12 Applications   60
List of Suppliers   62

INTRODUCTION

Découpage is the creative art of decorating hard surfaces with paper cut-outs. It's title is derived from the French word 'découper' — to cut. The original concept was to submerge a cut-out under many coats of varnish to make it look as though the image had been inlaid in an object's surface.

The art of découpage flourished in 17th century Venice, and later experienced a resurgence in the French courts prior to the 1789 revolution.

Varnish imitating lacquer was invented in Europe in the 17th century and was prepared from resin-lac or shellac. The painted furniture industry thrived in Venice and master painters created impressive designs and etched them onto furniture. The time consuming colourings were later applied by apprentices.

Mass production of the master painters' original designs (hand-coloured by the apprentices) allowed them to be cut out and glued onto prepared surfaces then varnished repeatedly to resemble the wonderful Oriental lacquered furniture. The layers of varnish disguised the pasted prints so that they appeared hand-painted.

At this time the major essence of découpage was classical and incorporated prints from Boucher, Watteau and Pillement and often découpage works favoured the chinoiserie style. Japanese and Chinese lacquer furniture of this style was the precursor of découpage and was introduced to Europe by the East India trade in the 16th century. This traditional style entailed hand-colouring black and white prints with artists' oils and is the method perpetuated by the purist American Découpage Guild.

During the Victorian era découpage was revived in a different form. In the 17th and 18th centuries Japanning was the English equivalent of découpage, however the most popular examples of the sentiment of 19th century work were the Victorian scrap screens. They were whimsical and this style is enjoying a new popularity today.

Hiram Manning reintroduced découpage to the world and his excellent work *Manning on Découpage* is an insrpiation to all who wish to achieve the beauty of such works of art without the usual prerequisite of painting skills.

All forms of découpage employ the same methods — the surfaces of objects to be découpaged have to be well prepared, images and object are sealed, pictures are cut out and assembled in a pleasing design and then are glued down separately, with the glue distributed evenly and the excess removed from above and beneath the picture. The design is then finely coated with up to 30 coats (and more) of varnish, sanded frequently to achieve a flat, smooth surface and waxed to produce a mellow finish.

Any hard object can be used for découpage — wooden boxes, chests, chairs and other furniture, ceramics, glass, metal and luggage, especially hat boxes. Quality assurance is essential. Every element must be worked in absolutely correct order to perfect the technique and every aspect has to be precisely executed. When this is achieved, your reputation as a serious découpage artist is assured.

People should be encouraged to do their very best to combine a classic design with a beautiful finish and not be satisfied with putting down a few images and slapping on just five or six coats of varnish. Anyone wanting to achieve a quick result with shortcuts will find this craft very frustrating.

Image suitable for découpage

When the techniques are perfected the main factor contributing to the success of a piece is the availability of pictures. These govern all your work and are the main tools in a project. The design is of next importance as it takes patience and a critical eye to position and superimpose the pictures to achieve a pleasing effect.

'Is it art or is it craft?' This perplexing question is often raised. It is like asking, 'Is it opera, light opera or a musical?' Both questions beg the response 'Is it relevant!' The tortured artist may never be satisfied with his work.

The concept of art will differ from one person to another, however my response to découpage which is beautifully composed and which has an ideal finish is that it must be art. Craft should not be a demeaning connotation. There is an element of both art and craft in découpage. Assembling the design is the art; executing a perfect finish denotes a craftsman. What is relevant is your enjoyment of the finished product.

Almost all previous texts on découpage follow the traditional method as espoused by Hiram Manning — preparing and sealing an item, painting the background with great care and then composing and gluing a selection of hand-coloured prints to this background. Rarely are the pictures superimposed.

My appreciation of découpage is that it evolved from the 'cutting' techniques. My design is more informal and more inventive, opting for an all-over pattern of everything and anything — a 'mille fleurs' technique.

Découpage is simple but you must pay attention to each element. When every step is followed meticulously you should have no need to refer to Chapter 11 — Problems and Solutions; however, recovery of a defect is also reasonably simple and this is highlighted in Chapter 11. Included in this book are detailed instructions for each of the techniques involved in découpage, instructions for a number of different projects and final finishes.

CHAPTER ONE

OBJECTS AND IMAGES

OBJECTS

Découpage can be applied to any hard, smooth surface. Wooden boxes, trays, chairs, tables, desks, picture frames and mirrors are ideal, as are hat boxes. Plastic, porcelain, metal, glass and leather require more extensive preparation. The range of items chosen for découpage can even be extended to violin cases, screens, chests of drawers and grandfather clocks.

It's best to start with a small object without hard edges, hinges and corners, such as a tablemat (a detailed description begins on page 30).

Practising on a tablemat enables the techniques of cutting and gluing to be mastered. From this starting point it is possible to venture on to small wooden boxes, then hat boxes, which require extra effort because of the scalloped edges and hinges.

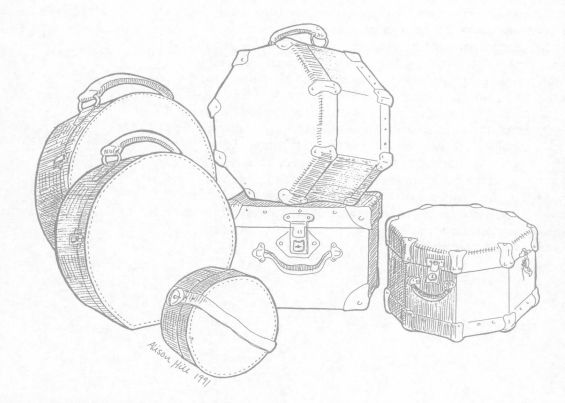

Boxes and old trunks are ideal for découpage

IMAGES

One of the most appealing aspects of découpage is the limitless range of imagery from which to choose. Selecting prints is very important. They should be beautifully defined and coloured as they are the major requirement of découpage. Consider restricting the number of prints when something is beautiful in its simplicity.

Ideally, prints for découpage should be on thin paper of consistent quality and colour. While wrapping papers satisfy this requirement, they need to be sealed to prevent 'bleeding'. They should be flat or rolled papers, not folded ones. The best pictures are those from books. Pages from glossy magazines can be used but again need to be sealed. Prints are also good but need to have the thickness of paper reduced. (See Chapter 3 — Techniques, 'Preparation'.)

I avoid embossed papers and cards, and usually disregard books and papers which are too porous as the quality of paper is unsuitable for découpage. Be wary of the papers which are extra glossy, and foils. Some other resources for prints are sheet music, childrens' picture books, artbooks (when selecting books check the number of colour pictures and the quality of the colour), photographs (can be laser colour photocopies), Japanese rice papers and postcards. Copies of images can be made using a laser colour photocopier but these pictures are particularly vulnerable to 'bleeding' and should be sealed several times on each side. I avoid photocopies as they do lose definition.

When selecting pictures for découpage it is a good idea to collate them into themes — actual and tonal. Clear plastic zip folders are perfect for this activity as they allow easy access and viewing. They eliminate the time consuming and frustrating searches for a particular picture. A theme list may be something like the following:

- Antiques
- Art
- Australiana
- Bears
- Black and White Prints
- Coins
- Dolls
- Fashion
- Flowers
- Interior Design
- Jewellery
- Music
- Oriental
- Religious
- Theatre, Ballet and Opera
- Victorian Scraps

Masculine themes can be produced with images of vintage cars, horse paintings, hunting etc.

The art section can also be divided into categories such as:

- General
- Egyptian and Greek
- Middle Ages
- Naive
- Flemish — Dutch 16th century
- Renaissance
- Italian
- French — 17th and 18th centuries
- Russian
- British
- Impressionists
- Art Nouveau
- Art Deco
- American
- Aboriginal Art (Dreamtime)
- Modern

Keeping files on favourite individual artists is another idea — Botticelli, Bruegel, Gainsborough, Reynolds, Boucher, Fragonard, Rubens, Rembrandt, Renoir, Klimt, Mucha, Pre-Raphaelites (especially Waterhouse and Rossetti) and Victorian painters. Keep the themes consistent and true to the genre by not introducing outside elements to specific genres.

Images suitable for découpage

Images suitable for découpage

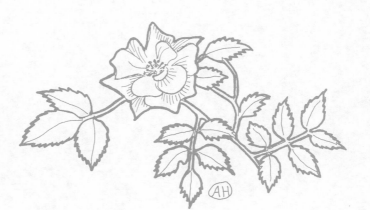

Images suitable for découpage

SEALING AND CUTTING

It is important to be familiar with these techniques before the pictures can be cut, and a design composed. (See Chapter 3 — Techniques.)

DESIGN AND LAYOUT OF PRINTS

Designing your découpage is very much the result of individual creativity. There are no hard and fast rules, and visual assessment of your efforts is the only true guide. You must be self-critical.

I select my object for its practical value to me, e.g a hat box which can be used as a briefcase or overnight bag. Then the theme should relate to the practical use of the item. It is essential to have a major picture which stands out, that is, your focal point or central motif. (Manning p. 47).

From this you build your tonal theme, i.e. you select pictures which compliment the colours of the initial focal picture, and you build your design around the focus, usually with smaller pictures which balance the original.

My style relies on classical art images and takes the form of compositional layering and superimposition. It may seem unrestrained, but there is a great amount of compositional control in each design.

All pictures must be assembled before the gluing process can begin. Blu-Tack is indispensable when organising a preliminary layout of pictures as the layout can be arranged and rearranged until the most appealing result is found. This way, satisfying results can be achieved rather than finding that the back of an object is superior to the focal area after it's too late. Once the layout is complete the pictures can be transferred to a large board (template) to ensure the design is not forgotten. Arrange the pictures to incorporate light, darkness and interest and create contrasts in the work.

When laying out a design always mark the top, bottom, back and front of an object. When working on a design for a box the most attractive pictures should be placed on the top and on the front and the less attractive ones should cover the sides, back and bottom. The focal pictures for hat boxes should be placed on the front and under the handle, leaving the less attractive ones for the sides and underneath. Before gluing, check that none of the images will appear upside down when the object is complete. Do not cut out images before sealing. Do not cut away the background until the picture is about to be used as it may be required when assembling the design.

It is important to ensure that no straight lines or picture edges are evident. This can be achieved by using flowers, leaves, tassels and jewellery to cover and soften the edges. Floral motifs are used extensively in découpage and add an extra dimension to art pictures.

Remember all pictures must be sealed before being cut out. (See Chapter 3 — Techniques, 'Sealing'.)

CHAPTER TWO

REQUIREMENTS

Découpage does not require a large outlay for materials; a basic kit (as outlined in this section) would cost around A$130. The bare necessities include cuticle scissors, a soft bristle brush and a wallpaper roller, pictures, an object to découpage, sealer, glue, varnish, sandpaper, Scotchbrite, steel wool and wax polish.

It is important to purchase a quality pair of scissors to give pictures good edges. The best cuticle scissors are those with fine, sharp, curved blades. Poor quality brushes shed hairs, so for varnishing opt for a soft bristled 2.5 cm (1 inch) brush that is synthetic sable. When applying sealer and gesso it is possible to use cheaper brushes.

Wallpaper rollers are optional but a 10 cm (4 inch) wide rubber roller with rounded edges is the best to purchase. (Those with hard, flat edges will cut into the print.) Manning recommends against using a roller as its hard surface can press out all the glue and leave none to adhere the picture to the box. But using a roller with a gentle pressure makes gluing a picture less time-consuming and gives a more even finish. Purchase glue, sealer and varnishes which are compatible because a reaction can dissolve the sealer. Also be careful when applying varnishes and resins on top of one another. Products which come in twin packs work as catalysts and will cut into varnish and produce a surface which resembles crocodile skin.

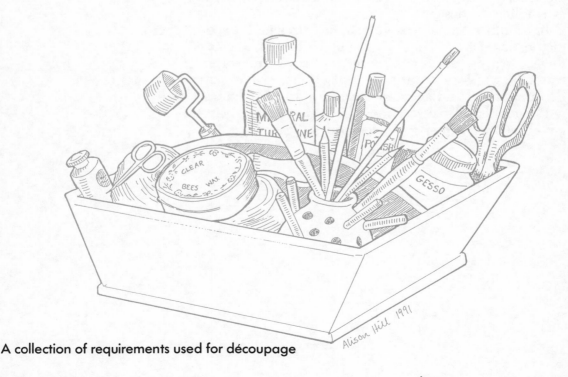

A collection of requirements used for découpage

Sealers are the insurance against 'bleeding' and prevent glue from seeping into wooden or porous surfaces. Liquitex Gloss Medium and Varnish, when used correctly, is 100 per cent effective as it has a creamy consistency. Matisse MM9 is also quite effective, as is an Atelier sealer. Aerosol spray fixatives are also feasible but should only be used on wrapping papers which have no print showing through. Micador and Asco workable fixatives can also be used for this purpose.

Glue is another important element in découpage and it should be strong enough to secure the print. Clag can be used on thin papers but it is preferable to strengthen it by combining one part PVA-Aquadhere to three parts Clag. Varnish should also be chosen with care and Walpamur Interior/Exterior Varnish (a traditional varnish) is preferable as it gives a mellow glow to work. Its only drawback is that it has a long curing time. There have also been excellent results with polyurethanes such as Dulux, Delta and Feast Watson.

The basic kit is a guideline only and can be extended as the découpage artist gains confidence and enthusiasm. The requirements list corresponds to each activity.

OBJECTS

Boxes, etc (see detailed projects and Chapter 1 – Objects and Images, 'Objects')

PREPARATION

Glass paper
Sealers (Liquitex and Atelier) and brush (cheap)
Gesso and brush (cheap)
Wood putty or Beeswax stick (does not shrink like
    other fillers)
Workable fixative
Tubes of artists' acrylic paints
Thin brushes
Rustguard for metal surfaces
Steelwool
Wet and dry sandpaper

CUTTING

Scissors: (i) curved cuticle
               (ii) long blades
Scalpel and blade
Plastic zip folders
Blu-Tack
Cardboard templates of object

GLUING

Clag school paste
PVA adhesive
Cheap brush
Wallpaper glue
Pen to sign work (either gold, fineline or waterproof)
Craft glue
Sponge
Towel and paper towel
Water and container
Rollers (10 cm/4 inch rubber is best)
Oil-based pencils (sepia, black, flesh)

VARNISHING

Imitation sable brush, 2.5 cm (1 inch)
Walpamur Interior/Exterior Varnish or Dulux
 Polyurethane
Tack cloth
Protective mask and goggles
Mineral turpentine
Brush cleaner

SANDING

Wet and dry sandpaper Nos 280, 400, 600, 1200, 2000
Steel wool, No 0000
Scotchbrite
Sanding block (rubber or cork)
Top Gear cutting compound

WAXING

Beeswax furniture polish
Goddard's Cabinet Makers Polish with Beeswax

BRASS LINING

Drill
Brass fittings
Fabric
No 10 cardboard
Wadding
Craft glue
Spray adhesive
Shears (for fabric)

ANTIQUING

Sealer
Patina
Surgical disposable gloves
Cotton squares or tissues
Burnt umber artist oil paint
Protective mask

CHAPTER THREE

TECHNIQUES

PREPARATION

The selection of objects and prints is outlined in Chapter 1. After the selection process there often needs to be refinements made to the image or object before sealing can take place.

Prints often need to have the thickness of paper reduced before they can be used for découpage. To do this, separate the corner with a fingernail, carefully pull the lifted paper to the opposite side and separate the back from the front. Several coats of sealer must be applied to the back of any print, postcard, photograph or card reduced in thickness in this way. If sealer is forgotten the porous new back of the print will cause a 'bleed' as soon as glue is applied. Remember that calendars, prints and thicker papers will require many more coats of varnish to submerge them.

Wooden objects need careful preparation as the wood, being porous, will absorb ('leach') glue and deprive the picture of adhesion. With little or no adhesion between the pictures and the wooden surface a great stress will build up after numerous coats of varnish have been applied and an air bubble will eventually form. This problem can be rectified (see Chapter 11 – Problems and Solutions) but it is preferable to eliminate the possibility of 'leaching' in the first instance. Protective sealers will guard against this.

Old wooden objects must be stripped so any paint, varnish or other surface is removed. Use a paint stripper if necessary and then sand the surface with glass paper and finish by sanding with No 280 wet and dry paper. All dirt, grease and wax must be removed with a mild detergent. The surface should be rinsed well, rubbed lightly with sandpaper and left to dry. New wood needs to have any imperfections filled. Apply the filler or beeswax stick generously to cracks, nail holes and scratches as the products shrink as they dry. Allow the filler or beeswax to dry, then sand lightly. Always wipe objects to remove dust before sealing them.

Gesso will also provide a smooth working surface. It is a whitening plaster compound which is mixed with glue and water and is available from art supply stores. It has a consistency resembling thickened cream and should be painted on after the wood has been cleaned. Apply five coats, alternating the directions, and be sure that each coat is thoroughly dry before applying the next one (about three to four hours is the usual drying time but Liquitex Gesso dries in minutes).

When the coats are complete, lightly sand the surface with No 280 sandpaper (dry), polish it with the finest steel wool, No 0000 if possible. When complete it should feel like smooth ivory, at which point sealer can be applied. A gesso surface is ideal to glue pictures to as there are no imperfections that will require extra varnishing.

Painted backgrounds can also be used but need to be sealed again before gluing pictures in place. (See Project 1 – Tablemat.)

Metal surfaces require meticulous preparation to guard against rust. Rust can be removed with a steel brush but this is a time consuming process and the result achieved by a sand blaster is superior. Once the sand blasting is complete a coat of zinc chromate or rusticide should be applied. Make sure that the bare hands do not come into contact with the surface or rust will form on any spot that has been touched. Use cloth or paper to protect the hands if touching or moving the object. A coat of sealer or paint can then be applied. There are commerical rust removers and converters available. Surface rust on the catches, hinges and handles of hat boxes and luggage can be removed with sandpaper or steel wool. Larger items such as trunks should be scrubbed with a good scouring powder then dried. Next rub them over with white spirit (methylated spirit), and wipe away dust and paint with a rust inhibiting paint such as Rustguard, which is a rusticide and epoxy enamel combined (no primer is required). Rustguard comes in a wide range of colours which will tone with the chosen theme colour and will cover the edges of hat boxes or trunks. After applying Rustguard lightly sand to remove dust and bumps and then apply a coat of sealer.

In preparing an object that has older hinges and closures (such as a cutlery box) try to remove the hinges to make preparation easier. Clocks are a challenge but the faces must be removed before beginning découpage.

DO NOT remove hinges, clasps and handles from hat boxes as refitting them causes no end of trouble.

SEALING

Sealer forms a protective base for découpage and should be used sparingly. If a print is not sealed and is stuck down, varnish will later seep into it and ruin the découpage. It is used to protect the objects and images and is used under and over practically everything. It will also prevent overall discolouration of the varnish. (Manning p. 77.)

Recommended sealers are mentioned in Chapter 2 – Requirements, and are listed in the basic découpage kit. Always seal prints before cutting them as cutting first will create curling edges. The sealer strengthens the paper by adding a plastic-like coating and prevents tearing and overstretching. It also prevents 'bleeding' (print showing through from the other side or an overall blotchy appearance).

Paint sealer sparingly on pictures or it will have a cloudy effect, but use it generously on porous boxes. Sealer is water soluble so it is very important to dry the sealer brush before applying another coat or the sealer will be broken down.

Sealer is used to coat images and objects

Acrylic sprays can be used to seal wrapping paper and should be applied to both sides of the paper. These sprays should not be used on magazine pages as there is not adequate protection against heavy print showing through. Laser colour photocopiers need several coats of sealer on the front and back. Use well-brushed-out, sparing coats and alternate the brushing direction for each coat.

Sealer is brushed onto the chosen object and onto each side of the images and then it is again brushed over the completed design. Before the last coat be sure all the surface glue is removed, that obvious edges have been coloured with oil pencils and that the work has been signed, if desired.

The sealer also protects the paper from discolouring greatly from varnish and makes cutting easier by adding body to the paper. It also protects the paper from becoming mushy during the gluing process and when cleaning off excess glue. (Manning p. 78.)

Place sealed cut-outs between sheets of waxed paper to prevent pictures sticking together when stored. Prints from good quality art books do not require sealing but the finished design should be sealed. The sealer is the insurance policy against subsequent frustrations.

CUTTING

Do not cut before sealing prints. Do not remove all background until you are about to use the picture – the background may be needed in assembling the design. Skilful cutting with a good pair of scissors is essential for a fine piece of découpage. The scissors for intricate cutting should be light and have fine, sharp blades and points, while those for cutting away excess paper should be straight.

Cutting out can become a very enjoyable part of the découpage process, after a little practise. The object is to remove all the white paper surrounds from a picture, leaving only colour. Use the large scissors to trim off the bulk of the white paper as precise cutting is difficult if the excess paper is not eliminated first. Define the shapes of the print with the small, curved scissors. Cutting neatly and accurately is very important as every tiny edge detail will show through the varnish of the finished box.

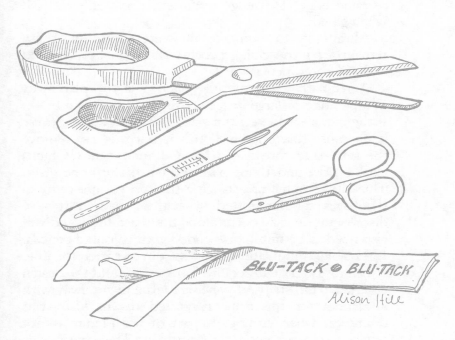

Good quality scissors are essential for découpage

Never use découpage scissors for cutting anything else and cut for one hour at a time only.

When cutting, allow the hands to relax and keep the wrists flexible. The object is to feed the picture through the curved blade, not to make a cutting action around the picture as such. Work with the curved blades pointing outwards as this gives a good edge. Always cut from underneath the paper, not from the top, so it is easier to see what is being cut away.

To cut, hold the print in the left hand (if left-handed the reverse is applicable) and keep the design on the left of the blade. Cut in an anti-clockwise movement, floating the picture through the scissors, ending at the same place as the beginning.

If interior sections are to be cut away do these before trimming the surroundings, as having excess paper around the design allows for easier handling. Poke a hole through the middle of the interior section with one point of the small scissors then bring the point of the scissors up through the bottom of the hole to cut away these areas. As the paper is moved through the scissors, open and close the blades smoothly, turning the print and wriggling it slightly to create a minute serrated edge. This edge turns under and adheres well when glued.

Always try to eliminate all white edges but if any remain after the gluing process they can be disguised with oil-based pencils.

A regularly encountered problem is the placement of a painting or large image across two pages of a book. If the picture is the central stapled page of a book there is no cause for concern. If this is not the case remove the staples or thread and leave about 6 mm (¼ inch) extra on the underlying page and cut the top one flush. This allows some area to glue the top picture onto so the pages can be butted up without gaps. Areas of discolouration may occur along the central line and will also need to be tinted or blended with coloured pencils. If possible, trail pictures over the join to soften the line.

Delicate areas will require 'bridges' to hold the design together. Thin strips of paper are left and cut away with a blade after the print is pasted down. Use your discretion when cutting. If part of the picture is not relevant to your design, eliminate it. The objective is form new designs from the original prints.

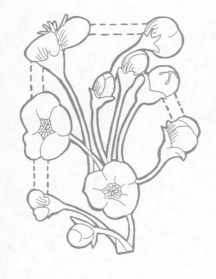

Cutting bridges for delicate areas of an image

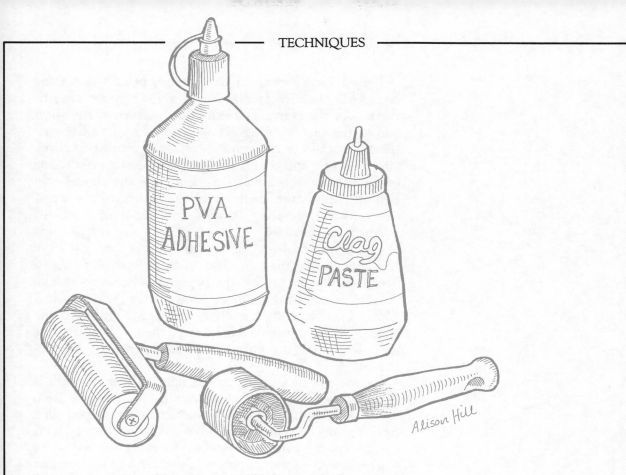

Rollers are used to eliminate air bubbles caused when gluing images in place

GLUING

Secure adhesion is the aim in découpage but every trace of glue must be removed from the surface before varnish is applied or a brown smear will form under the varnish.

The glue should not dry too quickly, to allow latitude in fixing the pictures and rearranging them if necessary. It should be transparent, non-staining and easy to clean off. Glue that is too sticky will cause tearing of pictures. Water-soluble pastes are the most suitable for découpage and a combination of three parts Clag and one part PVA-Aquadhere is the most suitable. Always apply glue to the hard surface rather than the back of the picture as it will moisten the paper and make it stretch and tear. Be generous with the glue as it is better to have too much rather than too little, and only glue one picture at a time. Smear the glue over the surface with the fingertips as it makes locating any small hard lumps and covering the surface area easier and gives a silky surface.

Keep a damp cloth close at hand, place the cutting onto the glued surface and add a little more glue to the top of the print. The extra glue acts as an emulsion and as the picture is sealed or of good quality the glue should not affect the print. Massage the print to allow air to escape and to encourage the glue to bond. Use gentle pressure on a roller to distribute the glue evenly behind the picture. Starting at the centre of the print use outward radiating strokes until all lumps and air bubbles are removed.

Check in the light for air bubbles. A cut will have to be made into the print later if an air bubble remains. To cut out an air bubble the paper should be dry. Make a slit in an unobtrusive place using a small, sharp scalpel blade. Gently probe the edges and apply glue into the space. Work the glue backwards then roll and press out. Touch up the cut with a colour pencil and seal the cut.

Check the découpage in the light to ensure there is not glue on the surface. Remove the excess glue with a well wrung out sponge. Wipe the glue from the roller. Seal sparingly. Difficult glue smears can be removed with a solution of a little vinegar or lemon juice added to warm water. Allow the glue to dry thoroughly – it must be completely dry before any edges are coloured. Pictures which lift, especially those at corners, will need thicker glue to persuade them to stick again. Sealer can be applied once more when air bubbles are removed. If another picture is to be added to a completed design, lightly sand the varnished area with No 000 steel wool, glue the picture down then continue varnishing.

VARNISHING

The fundamental rules of varnishing are good ventilation, good light, a dust-free environment and always wear a mask. (It's a good idea to have a fan operating or work with the windows open to allow the fumes to escape).

The weather is the predominant factor in varnishing, and rain, damp and high humidity can create a 'bloom' (the shine of varnish spoiled by a misty effect). Always varnish away from sunlight.

The varnish makes designs come alive — the result after one coat of varnish is quite notable. The aim of varnishing is to submerge the design so that the edges of the pictures disappear into the varnish and that they

THREE LEAF VICTORIAN SCREEN AND HAT BOXES
This stunning screen and series of hat boxes show how strikingly beautiful
découpage can be. Photographed at 'Roseville' Restaurant, a National Trust
listed building of the Australian Heritage Commission.

SMALL VICTORIAN SCREEN, OVAL WAXED BOX, HAT BOXES AND SHOE TREE
The hat boxes are composed from a *Victorian Scrapbook*
and *Forget-Me-Nots* book.

FRENCH SCREEN, HAT BOX, TRUNK AND FRAMED MIRROR
The ornate French screen features seventeenth century prints by Boucher,
Gainsborough, Winterhalter and Hogarth. Gainsborough's daughters
are depicted on the hat box.

HAT BOX, JEWELLERY BOX, SMALL BOX, HAND MIRROR, VASES AND GOBLET
The scalloped edges of the hat box frame the work of Gainsborough. The hat is
by Beh-Nielson. A print of 'Bubbles' by Millais is the focus of the jewellery box
and tiny flowers festoon the mirror, vases and wooden goblet.

WOODEN BOX
Nudes by Francois Boucher, Peter Paul Rubens, Hogarth, Lely, Watteau
and Titian adorn this box.

A VARIETY OF OLD WOODEN BOXES

TWO HAT BOXES AND A JEWELLERY BOX
The larger hat box features the Calmody Children by Sir Thomas Lawrence and
the small hat box is a collection of Victorian cards and memorabilia.

BROOCHES
by Nerida Singleton

COLLECTION OF DECOUPAGE BROOCHES, EARRINGS AND HAIR ACCESSORIES
by Amanda Ho

DECOUPAGE EGGS IN A COIR NEST

VIOLIN CASES
These feature European flower paintings from the sixteenth to nineteenth
centuries: Johann Wink, Ambrosius Bosschaert the Elder 1573-1621,
Henri Fantir-Latour 1836-1904, Jan Van Huysum 1682-1794,
Hendrik Reekers 1815-54 and Nicolaes Van Verendael 1648-90.

DOLL HAT BOX AND HEXAGONAL HANDBAG WITH A BACKGROUND OF DRIED ROSES

can no longer be seen or felt. This is the point at which the paper, design and object become one and exude an inner glow.

Traditional varnishes take at least six months to cure properly and should be treated with extreme care as the surface will mark easily. This type of varnish lends an object a mellow glow which is not present in fast drying polyurethane glosses. This yellowing effect ages the découpage and melds the tones in the pictures. With traditional varnish white pictures become ivory, pink tends toward orange and light blue assumes a greenish hue. To keep an integrity of colour opt for the polyurethane but never use quick drying glosses if the weather is bad as they may cause clouding.

Varnishing requirements include oil-based pencils and paint for touching up works

Purchase varnish in small quantities as it deteriorates quickly. When not varnishing regularly invert the tin so the skin will form on the bottom rather than the top. Never shake varnish as it promotes air bubbles and make sure lids are firmly sealed so air cannot enter. Always use a good quality, fine brush, even when varnishing large objects, as large brushes form thick coats, create obvious brush marks and promote a heavy build-up of varnish at corners and edges. Wider brushes also collapse in the middle, so there is no control of the thin spread of varnish.

Use a Tack rag to remove the surface dust before commencing varnishing. Place only half the bristles in varnish and be careful not to overload the brush. Use light, even strokes and brush horizontally from left to right. Try to brush the varnish out as much as possible to give an even thin coat. Do not brush backwards and forwards as this encourages air bubbles. Be certain no area is missed and no excess varnish remains. Working in good light will ensure the coverage of an object. After varnishing draw the brush up against the lip of the tin to remove all residue, then using the very tip of the brush give light, quick sweeps across the surface, moving from side to side. This minimises air bubbles and removes excess varnish, leaving just a thin film. To avoid definite brush strokes at the edge of the work lift the brush at the end of long strokes. Leave the object to dry in a dust-free place with good ventilation. A coat of varnish should only be applied every 24 hours. Change directions with successive coats.

When varnishing, change directions with successive coats as illustrated

Between coats keep the brushes suspended in turpentine so the bristles do not accumulate sediment and lose their shape. Always clean the surface of an object with a Tack rag before applying a new coat of varnish and remove excess turpentine from the brushes. Change the turpentine when it becomes clouded, or it will solidify. If a bristle becomes embedded in varnish do not remove it with fingers or the brush but catch the middle of the bristle with a needle and carefully ease it out.

Boxes need extra attention when varnishing. Do the top then the sides. Draw out the varnish, check for drips and eliminate the build up and runs which form on the top edges by repeating the drawing out process of the varnish on edges and corners. Apply several coats of varnish or sealer to the inside of wooden boxes before sanding, as the wood is very porous and will absorb the water used when employing wet and dry sandpaper.

Varnishing a hat box follows the same principles, with a couple of exceptions. Do not get varnish on hinges or clasps, do not varnish the inside top edge or the hatbox will not close properly. Alternate the direction of each coat and, if possible, hang the box from a hook to allow for drying. Clean brushes regularly with brush cleaner to preserve them.

SANDING

Sanding is only carried out when there is a good depth of varnish covering the images. Manning definitely states there needs to be 20 coats of varnish to feel confident that sanding will not destroy the prints beneath.

Sanding is the remedy for the lumps, bumps and crevices which start appearing in découpage after varnishing. If using polyurethane gloss it is possible to start sanding with No 1000 or 1200 wet and dry sandpaper after 10 coats but if using traditional varnish wait until 20 coats have been applied before starting and wait until 30 or 40 have been applied before using the finest paper, No 1200 or 2000. Vigorous sanding can cause problems such as shearing off corners and edges which are the most vulnerable areas on objects.

Before commencing sanding check the varnished surface of the object is dry by pressing it with a finger. If an impression is left then wait another day before beginning sanding.

When it is dry wrap a piece of No 600 wet and dry sandpaper around a cork or wooden sanding block and add a few drops of water to the surface of the object to create emulsion. Rub the sandpaper block over the surface in one direction (side to side or up and down). Do not use a circular, scouring motion as this will create scratching.

Regularly change the direction of sanding. Keep water close at hand to assist with emulsion. Sand until there are no evident dents or depressions. Dry the object and wipe with a Tack rag. Continue varnishing. If a white edge appears, stop sanding, allow to dry then colour the edge with an oil-based pencil. Seal again and continue varnishing. Avoid sanding this area until the coats have again built up to a good depth.

The aim of sanding is to create a uniform thickness of varnish over the entire object by removing the top surface of the most prominent picture. Each additional coat of varnish fills the crevices between the pictures and brings a flat and even finish to the surface. This can take anywhere between 30 to 100 coats and the more coats applied the deeper the varnish and the warmer the glow created.

From coat 20 to 28 use the No 600 sandpaper. After coat 28 use the fine No 1200 sandpaper until after coat 30. At coat 30 decide if the surface is to be glossy or waxed satin. To judge how many coats to apply check

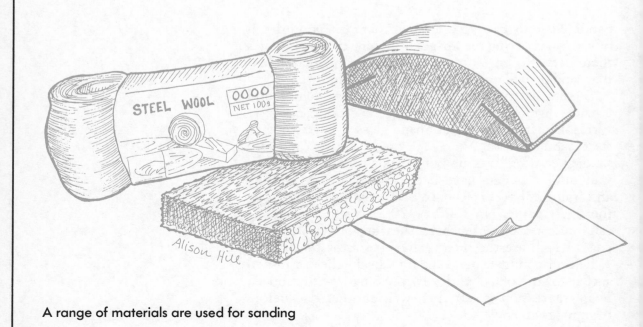

A range of materials are used for sanding

that all the shiny spots have been removed as these indicate the surface is not flat. Shiny spots will remain evident under a waxed finish.

To remove, use dry Scotchbrite and rub in the one direction. Alternate the direction and rub again. If the Scotchbrite is not successful then use the finest grade steel wool No 000 or 0000 (available from hardware stores or French polishers). Polish with the steel wool (dry) using very light pressure. Then use the No 1200 sandpaper again (wet) to remove any scratches. The finished surface should be uniformly dull.

It is important to remove the build up which occurs at the top and bottom rims or the box will not fit together. Remove the build up carefully with a scalpel blade or a vegetable knife. This process requires a steady hand as too severe a paring can cause the varnish to tear. (The remedy for this is to re-glue with craft glue and go back to varnishing with at least 10 coats to submerge the tear.) Once this is complete the inside of the rim can be painted with an acrylic paint to match the exterior pictures and interior lining.

Never use an electric sander.

CHAPTER FOUR

FINISHES

GLOSS

To achieve a final gloss finish indulge in a fresh tin of varnish and a new brush. Work in a dust-free environment and do not draw the brush up the rim of the varnish tin as it promotes air bubbles. Break down the varnish to seven parts varnish and three parts mineral turpentine. This allows the application to flow on more freely (Jennifer Bennell [*Master Strokes*, Hutchison, Australia, 1988] kindly supplied this information).

This must be the smoothest coat of varnish so use light quick strokes, feathering the brush back into the wet area. Do not brush backwards and forwards but in one direction only.

When the surface is covered, tip the brush lightly from end to end quickly so there are no air bubbles, brush marks, strokes or ridges. Next work on the sides, horizontally at first, then pull the varnish down, ensuring there are no runs at the edges or corners. Allow several days for the varnish to dry before fixing brass fittings and lining.

WAX

A perfect waxed finish is to be prized. Apply three thin coats of satin or matt varnish to your découpage, one coat every 24 hours. When it is dry, polish extremely lightly with wet and dry sandpaper No 1200 (wet) and No 0000 steel wool (dry). The aim is to create a uniformly dull finish and an utterly smooth surface. Leave several days before waxing.

Apply the wax in a thin coat with a soft, lint-free cloth, taking time to spread the wax evenly on the surface. Work on a small section at a time (about 2.5 cm/1 inch square), warming the wax first. I put a teaspoon of Beeswax and a teaspoon of Goddard's Cabinet Makers polish on a saucer and warm in a microwave oven on *high* for 20 seconds. Rub a damp cloth over the surface in a brisk circular motion. (Do not leave the wax to dry for too long or it will become difficult to work with.)

Polish the surface being worked on with a dry soft cloth. Each section may need another coat of thin wax which should be let dry and polished again. Waxing should result in a hard, glass-like surface which will resist dirt.

If the finished wax surface is unacceptable, wipe with turpentine, wash with detergent and rinse. Sand again with No 1200 wet and dry sandpaper and apply more coats of varnish if necessary. Then repeat the procedure of sanding (use Scotchbrite and steel wool to remove shiny spots if necessary), matt varnishing and polishing with steel wool. After the brass fittings are secured, lightly polish the surface with Goddard's Cabinet Makers Polish with Beeswax. Rewax regularly with Goddard's to retain the silky finish.

Waxing gives an object a silky smooth effect

CHAPTER FIVE

PROJECT 1
TABLEMAT

Working on a tablemat as a first project allows the basic techniques of découpage to be mastered. It entails gluing onto a flat surface so the problems of corners and edges, which are encountered on boxes, are alleviated. It is possible to devote attention to cutting, assembling the design and gluing onto a one dimensional plane.

METHOD

1. Lightly sand and remove any dust. If the tablemat has a coarse texture apply gesso with a 2.5 cm (1 inch) brush. (Liquitex gesso dries in minutes.) Some other varieties can take several hours to dry thoroughly.

2. Draw the gesso out evenly, and reapply by brushing in the opposite direction. Turn the board in clockwise revolutions to achieve an all over coverage. Lightly sand with No 600 wet and dry sandpaper (dry) between each application.

    Polish with No 0000 steel wool on completion. You may need two or three coats depending on the depth of texture in the surface. With some old surfaces you may need up to 10 coats to fill the indentations (e.g. crocodile skin, like the texture on a hat box). When used in this way gesso provides an ivory or marble surface and this is a joy to work on when adhering your images. It also eliminates the necessity of many more coats of varnish and constant sanding to achieve a surface that is thoroughly smooth.

3. Apply a sparing coat of Liquitex or Atelier Gloss Medium and Varnish, which acts as a sealer. Glue will not then penetrate into a wooden surface, which tends to be very porous. It is also essential to apply the sealer if you have previously applied gesso, even though the gesso itself acts as a sealer over wood.

If you have a smooth, shiny surface to seal, apply two coats of sealer in opposite directions. Again use sparingly so the sealer doesn't build up lumps and bumps which will cause problems under your pictures.

Allow each coat to dry before applying the next. Use a brush or sponge applicator which is not damp to apply the sealer. Towel dry the brush or applicator to remove excess water as this will break down the effectiveness of the sealer.

4. If you wish to paint a background, use artists' acrylics. Apply evenly in one direction. When dry, apply a second coat in the other direction. Seal when dry, as the acrylic paint is water-soluble and will smear when gluing the pictures in place. A sea sponge can create an interesting surface effect, giving an extra dimension to the work. When choosing paint select a colour sympathetic to the general theme of the design. Black may be chosen to add contrast or to emphasise the images.

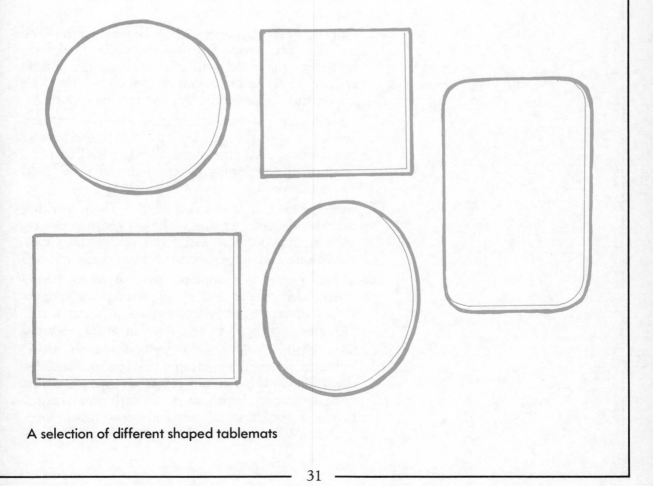

A selection of different shaped tablemats

5. Choose your focal picture, being sure all images have been sealed before cutting them. Compose your design in an effective way. (See Chapter 1 – Objects and Images, 'Design and Layout of Prints'.) Cut the pictures and arrange on a template to attain the overall effect of the design. (See Chapter 3 – Techniques, 'Cutting' for more details.)

6. Start by gluing down the focal picture. Glue each image separately and be sure each is secure and has no air bubbles or excess glue underneath before proceeding to the next picture.

7. Using a roller and a very light pressure, roll out the picture using long strokes, radiating them outwards from the centre of the image. Continue gluing images in this manner.

8. Covering the mat with wrapping paper is another background option. When applying wrapping paper, first seal it on both sides. (Wrapping paper can be sealed with spray fixative or sealer.) Press the edges of the wrap over the edges of the tablemat, turn the paper over and there will be definite impression lines.

9. Cut the wrapping paper slightly larger than the lines to allow for errors. Because the paper is already sealed it is less likely to stretch when the glue is rolled out. It is important to remember that the paper must be sealed before any cutting is done.

10. Place a generous amount of glue onto the mat and spread it over the surface with the fingers, being careful to spread glue along all edges and corners. Position the wrapping paper on the mat and add more glue on top to give emulsion.

11. Massage the glue with the fingertips, then, working quickly and using a roller with very gentle pressure, start rolling out the glue from under the paper. (Continue gluing, following the instructions above.)

12. When gluing is complete, remove excess using warm, clean water and a well wrung out sponge. Add a little vinegar or lemon juice to water if surface glue is difficult to remove. The surface should have no dull patches when observed in good light.

13. When dry, pencil any whitened edges and smudge them slightly if the colour is too obvious a contrast with the images. Sign your work with a waterproof pen or a gold fineline pen and spray lightly with fixative. When dry, seal the entire surface again.

14. Apply a coat of varnish, brushing in one direction only. Place the loaded varnish brush in the centre of the mat and draw the varnish out to each side. The object is to aim for thin coats. Tip brush to remove any air bubbles. (See Chapter 3 – Techniques, 'Varnishing' for more details.)

15. Allow to dry in a well ventilated, dust free environment. Apply only one coat each day. Wipe the surface with a Tack rag to remove any accumulated dust particles, then varnish once again, in the opposite direction. Apply 20 coats of varnish before sanding.

16. Sand with No 600 wet and dry sandpaper after each coat until you attain 28 coats. Change to No 1200 and polish after each coat to 30 coats. No 1200 sandpaper is finer and polishes the surface rather than being abrasive. (See Chapter 3 – Techniques, 'Waxing' for more details.)

17. Give a final coat of gloss varnish, being aware of air bubbles and surface dust and brush strokes which would impair your surface.

18. If waxing the mat, give three coats (one each day) of satin or matt varnish. Rub gently with No 0000 steel wool. Apply beeswax and buff to a gentle sheen. (See Chapter 3 – Techniques, 'Waxing' for more details.)

CHAPTER SIX

PROJECT 2
BOX

Choose boxes for their practical application. Always keep the focus of the design on the top and front of the box with less emphasis on the bottom and sides. The background can be painted, covered with wrapping paper (see Project 1 – Tablemat for details) or constructed from pictures. Choose images which are appropriate to the theme and the personality of the recipient (include favourite photos, flowers, etc).

Set out the design on a template using Blu-Tack to secure the pictures and ensure there are enough images before commencing gluing.

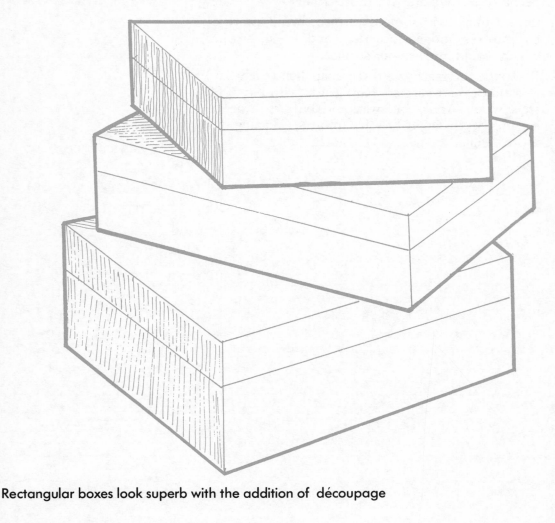

Rectangular boxes look superb with the addition of découpage

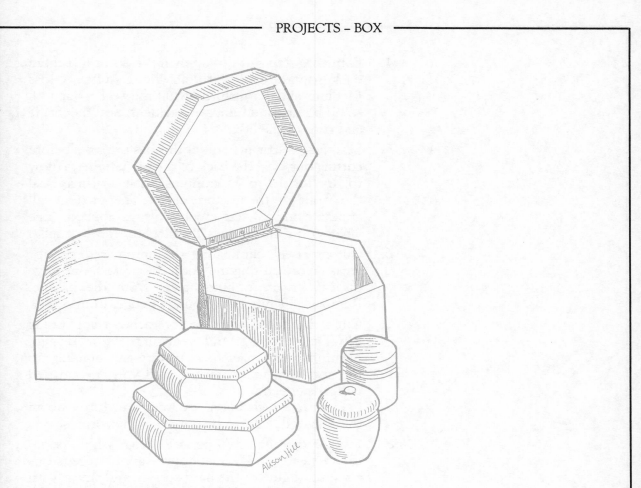

You can découpage boxes of many interesting shapes

METHOD

1. Mark the top and bottom of one side of box (inside) to ensure it will fit flush when hinged. Check for crevices which may need to be filled with beeswax stick or wood putty. Apply filler with a spatula. Be generous with the filler because it shrinks as it dries. Beeswax is the preferable material for filling as it does not shrink.

2. Sand the box well with glass paper then lightly with No 280 wet and dry sandpaper, and wipe clean.

3. If desired apply gesso before lightly sealing. Or, if desired paint the background with artists' acrylics at least twice, applying each coat in different directions.

4. Eliminate step 3 if not applying gesso or a painted background. Seal with acrylic Liquitex Gloss Medium and Varnish, drawing the sealer out well so no bumps and lumps are evident. Seal the inside and rims of the box.

5. Seal images sparingly on both sides of paper before cutting out. Seal the back of the picture first. Allow to dry for 10 to 15 minutes, then sparingly seal the front of the picture again. The picture will appear cloudy if too much sealer is applied. (See Chapter 3 – Techniques, 'Sealing' for more details.)

6. Cut precisely, eliminating the unrequired interior areas before cutting the outline. Cut with the curve of the scissors pointing away from the picture. Remove all white background at edges of image.

7. Cut a cardboard template for each surface. Using Blu-Tack arrange and rearrange your design, beginning with your focal picture and building up the complementary images until you are satisfied with the effect.

   Pictures which cover a corner and travel down the sides will have to be mitred at the corners.

8. Using a mixture of 75 per cent Clag (school paste) to 25 per cent PVA adhesive, apply a generous amount of glue to the hard surface and smear with fingertips until silky. Be sure there are no areas that have no glue or have lumps of hard glue before putting the pictures down. Massage with a little extra glue on top of the picture, until the glue becomes tacky and bonding between the picture and the surface takes place. The glue needs to be distributed evenly behind each picture.

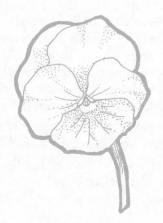

9. Add a little more glue and using a 5 cm (2 inch) or 10 cm (4 inch) rubber roller, roll with very gentle pressure from the centre of the picture and radiate out to edges. Hold work to the light to check if there is any accumulated glue or air behind the picture. Don't use too much pressure when rolling as this will eliminate all the glue and there will be no adhesion. Wipe the glue from the roller as it builds up.

10. Using a damp sponge wipe the excess glue from the surface of your picture. Glue will appear dull when held in the light. *Do not glue over a wet picture.* When all images have been glued down be sure there are no dull patches as these will appear as brown smears under the varnish.

11. Allow to dry, then check each image for white edges. Colour with an appropriate oil-based colour pencil (I mostly use sepia or black) and smudge edge if the line is too definite. This allows all the images to blend together and not be obviously separate.

12. Sign and date your work with a waterproof pen. If using a gold fineline pen, spray sparingly with workable fixative when ink is dry, otherwise it will smear under sealer. Allow fixative to dry.

13. Sparingly seal all surfaces. If you aren't able to finish gluing and have to leave the project overnight, clear away all glue and pencil any edges, and then seal the object. This prevents the pictures from losing adhesion, especially at corners, and also alleviates the possibility of gremlins enjoying a feast of the glued pictures. (Vermin are instantly attracted to the excess glue on the pictures.)

14. If you don't use all your sealed images, place them between sheets of waxed paper and file them into plastic zip folders. The sealer will compact them together if you don't use the waxed papers.

15. Use your protective mask and have good ventilation when varnishing. Varnish with a fine imitation sable brush, beginning at the top and using light sweeps in one direction. Do not stir varnish or polyurethane unless advised in the directions. Satin, matt and water-based products must be thoroughly stirred to incorporate the sediment. Gloss is a harder and more suitable product.

16. Where the top and sides of a box join, be sure to brush out any accumulation of varnish which builds up. Check for drips. Do not allow a thick build up of varnish at rims. Wipe excess varnish from brush on to the side of the varnish tin. Then using the tip of the brush lightly sweep across all surfaces to remove air bubbles and excess varnish. Work in a good light. Place both sections of box on tins to allow air to circulate about them to dry.

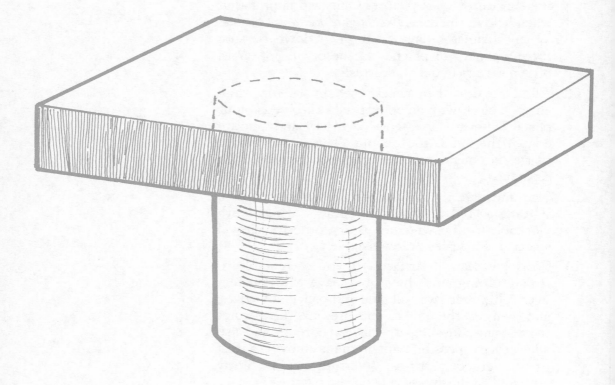

Elevate a varnished box to aid drying

17. Allow 24 hours drying time between each coat of varnish. Before reapplying varnish wipe surface dust particles off with a Tack cloth. Re-varnish, alternating directions with each coat.

18. When 20 coats have been applied, begin sanding with No 600 wet and dry sandpaper. Sand lightly in one direction with sandpaper (wet) wrapped around a rubber or cork block. Wipe off the white residue with a damp sponge, dry, then go over any white edges showing on images. Colour edges, seal and begin varnishing again.

19. Repeat the sanding process using No 600 wet and dry sandpaper until surface is quite flat. This may take somewhere between 30 and 50 coats of varnish.

    Change to No 1200 for the final polishing after the last three coats of varnish are applied. Remove the excess build up of varnish at the rims of the box using a scalpel or paring knife.

20. Be sure the surface is uniformly dull. (This means there are no crevices between superimposed pictures which show tendrils of gloss). If gloss is still evident rub with a dry Scotchbrite then No 0000 steel wool. Cutting compound is also helpful at this stage.

21. If wanting a gloss finish, apply a light coat of varnish broken down to seven parts varnish and three parts mineral turpentine. Be sure there are no air bubbles in the surface and place the object in a dust-free environment to dry. (Repeat this process until the surface is perfectly smooth.)

22. For a waxed finish, put a teaspoon each of clear beeswax and Goddard's Cabinet Makers polish in oven or microwave and warm (about 20 seconds on *high* in the microwave). Apply sparingly with a dampened cotton cloth (muslin) and work only small sections at a time. Wattyl Danish Wax is also a recommended product. Dip the cloth in boiling water and buff each section before moving to the next one. Repeat if necessary. Apply a final light coat of Goddard's over the entire surface and repeat this often during the curing time to enhance your object. It can take 6 to 12 months for an object to completely harden.

23. Using an electric drill and $5/64$ inch bit, secure brass corners. Never select fittings which are secured by nails, the ones with screws are the most suitable. Use a $5/64$ inch drill bit for all the fittings and start with the corners. Next work on the handle and then the top. It is easier to manipulate the fittings before the hinges have been attached.

    To attach the hinges, measure an equal distance from the ends and drill opposite sides in sequence. Add the clasp last and choose one that has a padlock. It is best to secure the top of the clasp and then line up the underneath section to ensure it is not too loose. An antique padlock and handles can add a great deal of style to a box.

24. Paint the inside of the box rims with artists' acrylics. Allow to dry. Apply 2 coats of sealer, allowing time to dry between coats.

25. Line with desired fabric. To line a box, cut 10 cardboard shapes (use No 10 white cardboard from newsagents or craft supply stores). You must allow room for the thickness of fabric at each side. Cut 6 mm (¼ inch) wadding the same size as the top and bottom, lightly spray card with spray adhesive and stick wadding to the card.

Cut fabric 1.5 cm (½ inch) wider than shape all around. Mitre the corners to allow fabric to fit flush at corners when glued, i.e. cut a triangle from each corner of fabric. Glue edges of fabric to back of cardboard with clear craft glue. Be sure the shapes fit snugly in the bottom of the box. Apply craft glue to the bottom of the box, and spread evenly with a spatula. Place shape onto glue and weight it to secure adhesion.

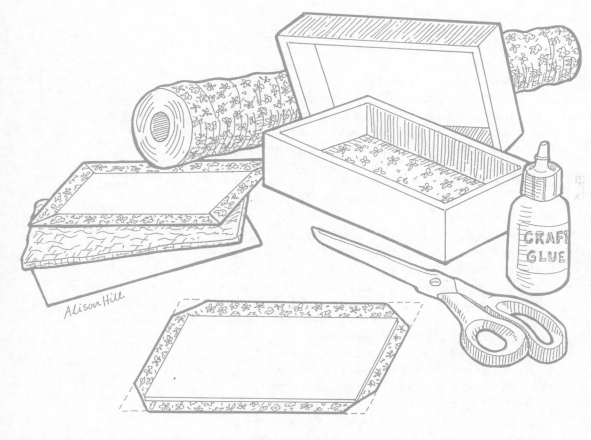

Lining a rectangular box with fabric is a simple process

Now that the thickness of card, wadding and fabric is determined in the top and bottom of the box, reduce the width of cardboard shapes for all sides accordingly. The length of the sides will also need to accommodate two thicknesses of extra fabric so keep readjusting them. Don't pad the sides as this reduces the interior space of the box. Repeat the procedure for the top and bottom, omitting wadding. Lightly apply spray adhesive and glue fabric to card. Mitre corners. Use craft glue to secure the edges of fabric to the card.

Do each side separately. Secure sides with craft glue. Keep pressure on them until adhesion is completed. Glue some ribbon behind one side of the lined card to prevent the box from falling back when open. I do these two sides last.

26. If your box is round or oval with the lip of the lid fitting over the base, make a pencil line around the base of the lip onto the bottom and only paste pictures to this line. Successive coats of varnish will build up and prevent the lid from fitting. The bare areas can be painted a colour which matches the background colour of the images or co-ordinates with the lining.

COVERING A BOX, USING ONE SHEET OF WRAPPING PAPER

Covering a box, using one sheet of wrapping paper, to give a background, has the same effect as painting a background.

To be accurate you need to cut a template from the measurements of your box. You will end up with a T shape. The top of the T incorporates the top and sides of the box. The trunk of the T accounts for the front, bottom and back. You must glue only one face at a time. When cutting your paper allow a little extra, as it can stretch and become misshapen.

You must work very quickly. Spread glue evenly on the top, place the centre section of the T down, roll out excess glue quickly, and be sure to remove excess glue from each edge with your finger or the glue will soften, stretch and perhaps tear the paper at that edge. You next tackle one side, rolling the glue out from the top. (You don't want a bulge of glue remaining where the top and side meet.) Be sure to get a firm impression of the join as this will aid you to locate it with your scalpel when the time comes to separate the box once it is completely dry. Use the same technique to do the other side, and repeat it with the front. Where the sides and front join, try to butt the edges, but if they aren't accurate wait for the paper to dry before snipping the papers flush with your curved scissors. Each other face is glued accordingly, and adjustments may have to be made if edges overlap. Don't be tempted to allow them to overlap — it is better to have securely glued, flush edges. Using the thickest part of the scalpel, prise it into one corner, and it should run smoothly through the join. The glue actually sticks the box together so you will have to gently lever it apart.

Always check your joins to be sure pictures are securely glued when you have separated the top and bottom with a scalpel. Re-glue where necessary.

Remove excess glue and seal in the usual way. *Never* paste any extra pictures over joins until the top and bottom have been separated with a scalpel. It is

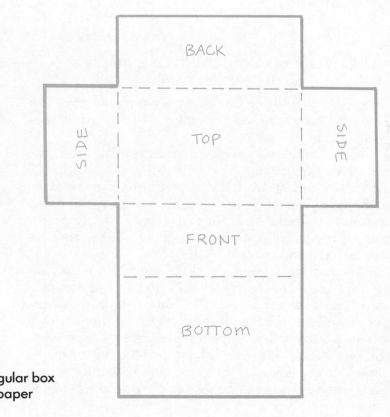

Pattern for covering a rectangular box with one sheet of wrapping paper

SOME OF THE MANY SOURCES OF IMAGES TO USE FOR DECOUPAGE
(see Chapter 1)

COMPLETED JEWELLERY BOX, AND SOME OF THE STAGES INVOLVED
(see Chapter 6)

Step 1
Cut out the image, using
good quality scissors with
a sharp, curved blade

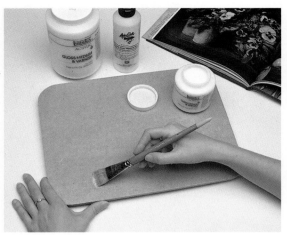

Step 2
Seal with a sparing coat of
Liquitex or Atelier Gloss
Medium and Varnish

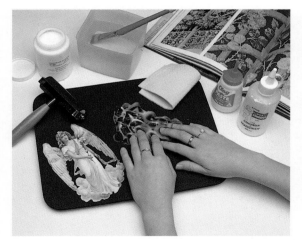

Step 3
Start by gluing down the
focal picture

Step 4
Roll out the picture, using
long strokes

COMPLETED HAT BOX, AND SOME OF THE STAGES INVOLVED
(see Chapter 7)

VARIETY OF EQUIPMENT USED FOR ANTIQUING OBJECTS LIKE THIS COLLAR BOX
(see Chapter 10)

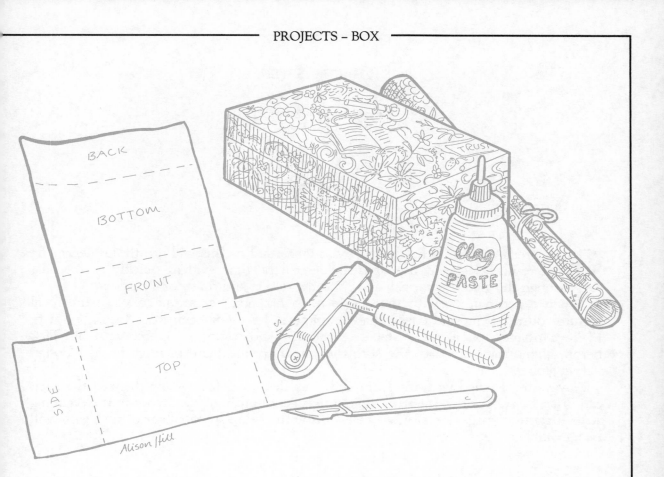

Covering a box with wrapping paper is a simple but striking alternative

impossible to find the join through more than one layer of pictures. Don't superimpose any pictures when the underlying pictures are still damp. This has the effect of separating the initial picture from the surface, and an air bubble will result.

If you have sealed your design and want to add another picture, then simply go ahead and glue it on. I often find spaces in my work after I have applied the first coat of varnish. Do not be deterred, simply rub the varnished area lightly with steel wool (No 000) and glue picture down, then go on varnishing.

Take care when you have a cut or blemish on your hands. Glue can penetrate and cause an infection, so wear surgical gloves if this occurs.

You will find that pictures which do lift, especially on corners, before you get a coat of varnish on to your design will need a thicker glue to persuade them to stick again.

CHAPTER SEVEN

PROJECT 3
HAT BOX

Good preparation of a hat box is most important as this will greatly influence the final result. Negligent use of rusticide will become evident quickly as the rust eats through the glue and varnish and ruins the design and finish of a hat box.

When experimenting with the design for a hat box be careful to place the focal pictures on the front and check that the pictures have not been placed upside down. Make templates for all the surfaces of the box and position pictures with Blu-Tack before gluing them in place. Be sure that there are adequate pictures for the design before gluing.

Always be satisfied with the front and back designs before gluing them as the back can often be superior to the front if attention is not given to the layout in the planning stage. Transfer images exactly as they are on the template or changes and gaps will be inevitable.

METHOD

1. Select a hat box which is firm and has a minimum number of depressions or warps. Remove the surface rust from all metal fittings – hinges, clasps, handle and studs. Sandpaper or steel wool (dry) will be appropriate.

2. Paint all metal surfaces, including interior metal rims, with a rusticide. This is very important. Allow to dry overnight. A second coat may be required but this can be done when hat box varnishing is completed, as the sanding technique often impairs the Rustguard finish.

3. If the hat box has a scalloped exterior the studs within the scallops will also need painting with Rustguard. Choose a Rustguard colour (Rustguard is a rusticide with an enamel paint) which matches your tonal theme and paint scallops, including a slight amount of the area within each scallop (in case your pictures don't fit entirely flush with the scalloped edges.)

4. Seal or gesso the hat box as has been described in Project 2 – Box. If the box has a very definite texture in its surface it will need many applications of gesso to ensure a smooth working surface is achieved. (See Chapter 3 – Techniques, 'Sealing' for more details.)

5. Paint background if desired; or

6. Select pictures with compatible backgrounds. Cover joins with appropriate smaller pictures to disguise straight lines. Arrange your composition on a template cut to the size of each surface.

7. Seal the images before cutting them.

8. Do not allow pictures to be glued beyond a pencil line's distance where the lip of the hat box fits over the bottom. There would be too much build up of varnish here to allow the box to close.

9. Place the pictures over the scallops, press firmly to make an impression of the scallop edges and points, turn the pictures over and, cutting from the back, trim the picture following the impression lines. This way the picture should slot easily into the point and curve of the scallop.

Hat box with scalloped exterior

10. The same procedure applies when needing to arrange your picture around hinges, clasps and handles. Firmly use a fingernail to define the outline of half of the clasps on the pictures. Cut away excess then replace the picture and define the clasps without cutting a section first.

11. For octagonal hat boxes and luggage with fitted corners observe the same procedure as step 10 to accommodate the picture around the corner metal shapes.

12. Glue pictures as described for previous projects. The only exception is that it is awkward to use a roller if the surface is not completely flat. You will need a lot of glue on the picture surface and use your thumb and a sponge to distribute the glue evenly behind your pictures. (See Chapter 3 – Techniques, 'Gluing', for more details.)

13. Wipe excess glue away.

14. Allow to dry.

15. Colour any white edges.

16. Sign your work and date it.

17. Spray your signature sparingly with workable fixative once the ink is dry.

18. Seal the entire surface.

19. Varnish the surface, using your protective mask, good light and ventilation.

20. Alternate the direction of brush strokes often. (See Chapter 3 – Techniques, 'Varnishing' for more details.)

21. Hang the hat box on a butcher's hook to dry – only applying one coat of varnish or polyurethane every 24 hours.

22. Use a Tack cloth to remove surface dust gathered between coats.

23. Begin sanding with No 600 wet and dry sandpaper (wet) after 20 coats. (Keep a daily record of the number of coats of varnish applied.)

24. Sand after each coat until the surface is flat and smooth and the picture edges are no longer evident.

25. Change to No 1200 sandpaper (wet) for the last three coats. (See Chapter 3 – Techniques, 'Sanding' for more details.)

26. I usually leave my hat boxes with a gloss surface. No dust or air bubbles please.

27. Wax, following instructions in previous projects. (See Chapter 3 – Techniques, 'Waxing' for more details.)

28. Touch up all metal fittings with Rustguard, if necessary.

29. Line the box with a thick fabric as the craft glue will 'bleed' through one which is too thin.

Requirements for lining a hat box

To line the box, place the box on No 10 cardboard and cut shapes for the top and bottom. The top will be larger than bottom as the lid fits over the bottom. Reduce the sides until the shape fits loosely but comfortably in the top and bottom of the hat box.

Measure the circumference of the top and bottom. Again the top will be larger. Measure the depth to the metal fitting. Add 2.5 cm (1 inch) to length and width. Fold down the fabric and glue a hem where the lining will meet the metal rim. Glue, beginning from the centre of the back and working in 10 cm (4 inch) sections. Hold fabric away from you so it does not attract glue. (Glue is hard to clean from velvet.)

Press the fabric against the sides and make a hem to overlap the join when the sides are secured. Repeat for the small rim in the top.

Cut 6 mm (¼ inch) wadding to the same size of bottom and top card shapes. Secure with spray adhesive. Cut velvet or similar thick fabric about 2.5 cm (1 inch) wider than the shape. Cut slits and glue the edge with craft glue. Put a lot of craft glue on the bottom of the box and weigh down the completed shapes. Repeat for top when bottom is secure.

Be very careful when working with craft glue and spray adhesive. Their fumes are extremely toxic and you need a mask and good ventilation.

Place some potpourri into the box to counteract the fumes of the craft glue when the box lining is completed, otherwise the fumes will remain overpowering for quite some time.

Small scalloped hat box with découpage design

CHAPTER EIGHT

SCREENS

Screens are the pinnacle of the découpage furniture process. Here the balance of the design is the most important ingredient.

A consistent and tonal theme must cover the panels. The choice of design for the scene will depend on the eventual surroundings, so consider these when planning a design, e.g. a modern design will not sit well in a period setting and vice versa. The panels will have to be removed before découpage can be added.

Designs for découpage screens are only limited by your imagination. As discussed earlier in the section on images all the themes mentioned can provide wonderful results. Perhaps the major side can have a Victorian composition and the reverse be simply covered with wonderful flower prints.

I have seen colour on one side with black and white on the reverse (though with age it became black and ivory). Silk can also be used on the reverse side. My conversation with an Adelaide découpage enthusiast revealed she has done a screen with authentic old scraps. The other method she employs is Japanning. Both of these sound remarkable.

Screens can have one panel, or up to five if you so desire. Fire screens are one panel only, as are the old nursery draught screens.

Remember that the many coats of varnish will extend the depth of the panels and this can prove awkward when replacing them. Ensure the depth of the frame is sufficient to contain the increased depth.

Victorian screens suffered from too few coats of varnish and the images came loose easily from the canvas on which they were pasted. Be sure of the finish of yours – the whole découpage process consists of the composition of images and an ideal or perfect finish.

This ornate single screen lends itself to period découpage images

An elegant two-leaf screen ideal for découpage

The larger central panel is the natural focus of this triple screen

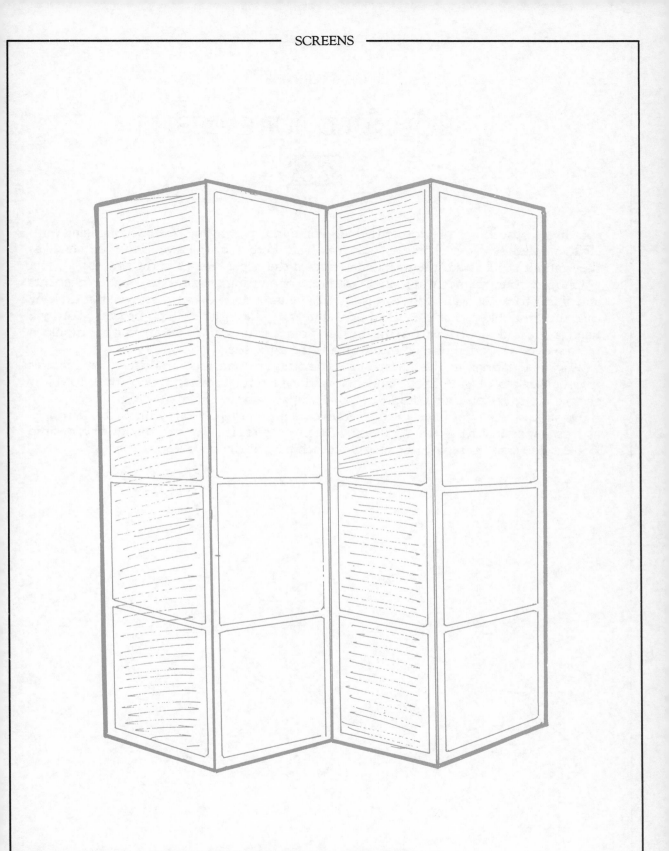

Choose découpage images to suit this modern four-fold screen

CHAPTER NINE

ROUNDED SURFACES

All the procedures previously defined come into play again when découpaging onto rounded surfaces. There is only one rule here – all pictures must be small as they cannot mould onto the rounded surface if the paper creases in the process.

Choose your theme using small pictures, or cutting pictures to smaller elements and gluing together again. Fine stems can be cut and trailed over the surface but extreme care must be taken that they do not disintegrate during the gluing process. You will need a great deal of glue on the top of your pictures if endeavouring to mould a picture over a wooden brooch disc which is the same size.

Any indentations in the surface of terracotta, etc. can accommodate your pictures if you use lots of glue above and below the picture. Press for some time to allow the picture to become almost mushy, so it will take up the shape of the surface.

Door knobs which have been découpaged are very popular. Paint a background, as it is impossible to secure a picture closer to the shaft. Buy two copies of a desired book if you want to repeat the images on each part of the door knobs.

A selection of small objects with rounded surfaces suitable for découpage

CHAPTER TEN

ANTIQUING

If you wish to achieve the effect of antique découpage, the obvious starting point is to locate old illustrations in print shops and museum bookshops, especially those of paintings which have become crackled with age.

This effect can be enhanced by applying general Bauernmalerai or folk art principles of sealing images, rubbing with an antiquing patina, covering the surface generously with burnt umber oil paint, allowing some time for this to accommodate to the print and then removing any excess oil paint to give the desired level of ageing.

Crazing is the irregular cracking or splitting of a painted surface. Painting before the previous coat had dried will produce this effect. If the crazed appearance is deliberately sought in order to imitate the cracks of antique decorated objects, there are quite a number of proprietary lines, e.g. Jo Sonya's Crackle Medium which is accompanied by directions. It would seem it is possible to crackle over a sealed image, antique the crackled effect, then varnish as normal. However my intention would be to use the crackle over the fully varnished product and then apply several more coats of protective varnish.

Prior to the availability of the patinas, the antique effect was achieved by substituting a special finish which was a mixture of linseed oil, pure gum turpentine and Turkey umber with an addition of some clear varnish. The mixture was brushed on and then immediate rubbed off with a soft cloth.

Below I have outlined two techniques which are borrowed from the dedicated Bauernmalerai artists, Diana Brandt and Glynne McGregor. Use oil-based artists' paints and oil-based patina for the best effect. The water-based ones are less efficient.

DIANA BRANDT'S TECHNIQUE

REQUIREMENTS

    Matisse sealer MM 12
    Patina Matisse MM 17
    Burnt umber oil-based paint
    Inexpensive coarse brush
    Surgical gloves (disposable) and protective mask
    Wax (if desired)

METHOD

1. Attach a picture to cardboard with non-stick
    adhesive tape.

2. Apply six coats of sealer to picture, brushing in opposite directions (cross-hatching). The coarse brush will give a linen-like appearance. Allow 10 minutes to dry between each coat, then allow 24 hours to cure all coats.

3. Place the picture in hot tap water for 30 minutes, putting it in a plastic container with a sealed lid, then remove and peel sealer back from the picture and separate.

4. Apply a coat of sealer to the object and let it dry, then apply a coat of sealer to the back of the picture and use it as the glue to stick the picture to the object. Be careful to position the picture correctly as it dries quickly. Trim the edges of the picture if it goes beyond the edge of the object and rub with sandpaper.

   Leave to dry for 24 hours then begin the antiquing process.

5. Wrap a rag around your fingers and dip one finger in patina up to first joint, then squeeze about 2.5 cm (1 inch) of burnt umber oil-based paint over the finger which was dipped in patina. Rub it onto the object with hard circular movements to totally cover it.

   Leave for about 10 minutes then rub off the paint in selected sections to give the desired antique effect. Take off as much as desired using a dry cotton rag. The curing time depends on the humidity and temperature. Allow to dry thoroughly before beginning the varnishing process, or wax with Liberon wax.

Antiquing can be used to disguise areas where the papers do not meet correctly at hinges and corners. Accentuate focal points by using the antiquing for relief work and perspective. It will tone down brightness and can blend with the background.

The overall effect is olde worlde and lends a burnished look to objects. Raw Sienna oil paint can be used if you want the finish to have a warmer quality.

GLYNNE MCGREGOR'S TECHNIQUE

REQUIREMENTS

Scottie's Antiquing Patina
Old singlet fabric for cloths
Liquitex Gloss Medium and Varnish Sealer
Tissues
Surgical gloves
Liquitex Burnt Umber oil-based paint
Mop brush

METHOD

(Always antique in a well-ventilated area, wear surgical gloves and when finished throw all trash in an outdoor trash can.)

This technique makes a surface look as though it has been darkened with age.

The surface to antique must be completely dry. For small, flat items, the entire surface can be done at one time.

1. Dampen a small, clean cloth with patina. Rub the entire area to be antiqued with this cloth, making sure all areas are covered, but not dripping. There should be an even sheen with no puddles.

2. Place a tiny dab of oil-based paint on the same area of the rag you used previously. Apply this to the surface using smooth, even strokes that start at one side and end at the opposite side – leaving no gaps in between.

3. Use a mop brush and brush the newly antiqued surface with long, sweeping strokes. Use a light touch and work from side to side without stopping. This removes any streaking caused when you applied antiquing mixture and softens the effect.

4. Use a clean rag to wipe the antiquing mixture off any areas that were painted in white or flesh tones. *Note:* A large percentage of the antiquing mixture can be removed if you don't like the effect. To do this, dampen a clean, cotton cloth with Scottie's Antiquing Patina and gently wipe the antiquing off.

5. When the antiquing is finished, allow it to dry at least one week before varnishing. If damp weather, wait nine to 20 days. Keep the object in a place where it won't smudge during the drying time.

6. Varnish as per instructions.

CHAPTER ELEVEN

PROBLEMS AND SOLUTIONS

If all the procedures outlined earlier in this book are followed then there will be little need to refer to this section. However, it is comforting to know that many problems can even be remedied at this late stage. A few of the more common ones are outlined below.

BLEEDING

This occurs if a picture is not adequately sealed. If this happens the only solution is to place another sealed picture over such a disaster, even if varnishing has taken place. This may disrupt the entire design. If you do not have another copy of the problem picture you will need to totally rethink your design.

Photocopies and prints may also appear to bleed if inadequately sealed.

Take a break, allow the picture to dry completely, and if your fears are resolved immediately put a sealer over the pictures and ensure that any extra pictures are completely protected. If unsure of a picture, paint front and back up to six times with sealer. Paint in opposite directions each time. This will then require a good adhesive, half Aquadhere to half Clag (school paste), as the paper is now much thicker.

GLUE BUBBLES

To remedy this, prick the pictures and allow the glue to escape. Allow to dry and when completely dry, colour in the discoloured area with an oil-based colour pencil. Seal before varnishing, or varnish will seep behind the picture.

AIR BUBBLES

Air bubbles under pictures will be obvious when pressed. Using a scalpel blade, make a cut in an unobtrusive place (preferably follow a distinct line). Lift each side of the cut and introduce Aquadhere into each area. Press the glue backwards then expel any excess. Repeat with the other side. Allow cut area to dry, then colour. I mainly use sepia, black, brown and flesh oil-based colour pencils. Seal and varnish.

Bubbles may also appear some time after varnishing. Use the same procedure, cutting through the varnish at an angle. More coats of varnish may be needed to disguise the cut if it is made near completion of an object.

WRINKLES

When varnish is applied too thickly this causes it to dry with a wrinkled appearance. This also occurs if you varnish when the weather is damp. Let the surface dry for at least a week, then re-varnish the object. The wrinkles will disappear with successive coats.

BLOOM ON VARNISH

This is a cloudly or milky effect which appears after you varnish on a wet or humid day. If you have enough coats to establish a depth of varnish to protect pictures, you can sand back, in fact sand that entire coat off.

If only a few coats of varnish have been applied there is no hope of sanding back without affecting your pictures. Strip them off and start again.

BUILD UP AND DRIPS

Take a scalpel to the dried varnish and slice it off at the varnish level. This will be sticky so allow to dry for some days, then continue varnishing. Don't try to sand this area or it will leave dark sanding marks.

SANDING THROUGH VARNISH

This happens most frequently on corners and edges. The sudden appearance of white paper is a huge concern. Stop sanding immediately. Colour with an appropriate oil-based coloured pencil, smudge, seal and continue varnishing. Avoid this area when sanding until the depth of varnish is uniform.

These problems illustrate how important it is to take all necessary precautions with sealers, glues and varnish.

CHAPTER TWELVE

APPLICATIONS

The possibilities for découpage are endless, only limited by your imagination. Time, patience and pictures are also factors, but assuming these are not too restrictive you can découpage for years, not becoming bored by repeating boxes or hat boxes. The following is a list of ideas for projects; doubtless you will encounter others as your interest in découpage grows.

- Tableware mats, teapot stands, trays, tea trolleys, tea caddies, wooden canisters and teapots
- Boxes – jewellery, sewing, trinket, knitting, fans, cutlery
- School cases
- Hat boxes – leather, compressed fibreboard (e.g. Globite), metal
- Luggage
- Music cases
- Trunks – tin and wooden
- Blanket and toy boxes
- Lap desks
- Plant stands
- Magazine racks
- Furniture – coffee tables, tables, chairs, sideboards, dressers, wardrobes, lowboys, bed heads
- Towel rails
- Frames
- Mirrors
- Screens and firescreens
- Ceramic and clay figures
- Pot plant holders
- Musical instruments and their cases – violin and guitar
- Handbags (hard leather or similar)
- Bathroom fittings
- Book covers (not padded)
- Albums

- Jewellery – brooches, bangles, earrings, hair clasps, belt buckles
- Door knobs
- Pepper grinders, rolling pins
- Gramophones
- Gourds
- Masks
- Wall panels, floors and ceilings
- Grand pianos – antiques (do not destroy the antique value of a beautiful item, avid découpers have to show some restraint!)

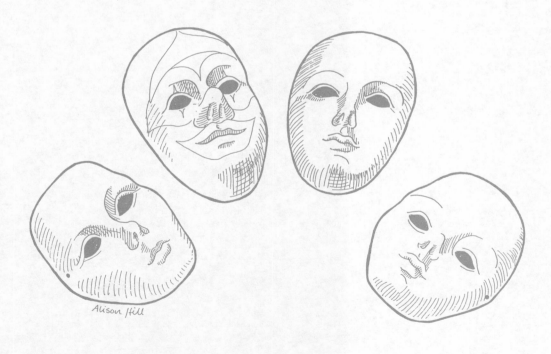

Masks can look very striking with the application of découpage